IF ANIMALS COULD TALK

EMBARRASSING
DADS

Quarto

First published in 2024 by Ivy Press
an imprint of The Quarto Group.
One Triptych Place, London, SE1 9SH
United Kingdom
T (0)20 7700 6700
www.Quarto.com

A catalogue record for this book is available from
the British Library.

ISBN 978-1-83600-100-3
Ebook ISBN 978-1-83600-101-0

10 9 8 7 6 5 4 3 2 1

Designer Cara Rogers
Editor Frank Hopkinson
Production Manager Rohana Yusof

Printed in China

FSC
MIX
Paper | Supporting
responsible forestry
FSC® C016973
www.fsc.org

Andrew Davies is the author of
many bestselling humour books
and series including *When I Were
A Lad*, *Sweary Cats* and the
Grumpy Handbook series.

Picture Credits
Alamy: Pages 6, 11, 16, 17, 27, 28, 32, 34, 39, 42, 58, 59
Shutterstock: Pages 4, 8, 12, 13, 15, 18, 20, 23, 25, 26,
31, 37, 41, 44, 45, 47, 49, 51, 52, 55, 57, 60, 62, 64
Cover: Shutterstock

IF ANIMALS COULD TALK

EMBARRASSING
DADS

IVY PRESS

INTRODUCTION

*I*f *Animals Could Talk...* is a celebration of the universal qualities of 'Dadness'. If you thought that embarrassing dads only existed on two legs, think again, because dads are the same throughout the animal kingdom. In the pages of this book, you'll meet a cat dad struggling with technology, a Jack Russell avoiding his in-laws, a penguin who won't admit he took a wrong turn, a raccoon barring the way to 'dad cave' and many, many more.

And what about dad dancing? It may be a crime against humanity but dads think their dance moves are like John Travolta, when everyone else thinks they've been stung by a wasp. Bears and lemurs, it turns out, are exactly the same. And if the family's watching TV together, guess who's in charge of the remote control...

Lovable and laughable in equal measure, prepare for a journey like no other through the diverse and delightful world of animal dads.

THEY LOVE A BIT OF DAD DANCING

"And sliiiiiide"

THEY NEVER FORGET IMPORTANT THINGS

**"Car keys,
car keys,
I knew I'd
forgotten
something"**

THEY LOVE TELLING THE SAME OLD JOKES

"Have you heard the one about the beaver and the data log...?"

THEY CAN BE SENSITIVE ABOUT BODY HAIR

"What do you mean I need to shave my ears...?"

THEY THINKS WIGS ARE HILARIOUS

THEIR POWERS OF MEMORY ARE LEGENDARY

**I definitely came down here for something – what was it?
I think it begins with 'S'**

THEY LOVE BEING RIGHT

"I HATE to say I told you so, but..."

THEY ARE NOT AT THEIR BEST IN THE MORNING

"This had better be good"

HE CAN'T WAIT TO SEE THE INLAWS WHEN THEY COME ROUND

“They’re STILL here...?”

THEY'RE ALWAYS UP FOR FUN

THEY'RE GREAT AT PUTTING UP SHELVES

THEY LOVE KIDS' PARTIES

"Beam me up, Scottie"

THEY LOVE TO GIVE AN AFFECTIONATE LITTLE HUG

"I love you so much"

THEY'RE A SOURCE OF CONSTANT EMBARRASSMENT TO THEIR KIDS

"Hey guys, does my fur look good like this?"

TECHNOLOGY IS THEIR MIDDLE NAME

"Maybe if I press all the keys, that'll turn it off"

THEY DON'T NEEDA SHOPPING LIST

"Hang on
a second –
did she say
get straw or
fish...?"

THEY LOVE COLLECTING BITS OF OLD WOOD

"This will come in handy"

SHARING IS CARING

"So that's 94 for me, and five for you"

"On second thoughts, is five too many?"

WHEN THEY SPRAY YOU WITH THE HOSE, IT'S FUNNY...

...BUT IF YOU SPRAY THEM, IT'S A TOTAL WASTE OF WATER

THEY'RE TOO COMPETITIVE AT SPORTS

"My ball! My ball!"

VERY FEW THINGS LEAVE THEM SPEECHLESS

"Have you REALLY emptied the dishwasher...?"

THEY LOVE GROOVING TO JAZZ

"Cool daddio!"

VISITORS TO THE DAD CAVE ARE ALWAYS WELCOME

"You're not coming in"

THEY JUST WANT TO BE DOWN WITH THE KIDS

"Gimme five, bro!"

SUNDAYS ARE RESERVED FOR DIY

...BUT NOT THIS SUNDAY. NEXT SUNDAY.

THEY LOVE TOILET HUMOUR

THEY ARE BIG FANS OF HOME DELIVERIES

"I love it when food comes to me"

YOU CAN'T GIVE THEM GOOD ADVICE

"What do you mean – that looks precarious?"

"It's as safe as hou... ou... ouses!"

...AND THEY PREFER DRAFT TO BOTTLES